Cambridge Discovery Readers

Level 1

Series editor: Nicholas Tims

Summer Sounds

Marla Bentley

CAMBRIDGE
UNIVERSITY PRESS

CAMBRIDGE
UNIVERSITY PRESS

79 Anson Road, #06-04/06, Singapore 079906

Cambridge University Press is part of the University of Cambridge.

It furthers the University's mission by disseminating knowledge in the pursuit of education, learning and research at the highest international levels of excellence.

www.cambridge.org
This American English edition is based on *Summer Sounds*, ISBN 978-84-832-3995-7 first published by Cambridge University Press in 2010.

© Cambridge University Press 2010, 2011

First published 2010
American English edition 2011

20 19 18 17 16 15 14 13 12 11 10 9 8 7 6 5 4 3

Printed in Great Britain by CPI Group (UK) Ltd, Croydon CR0 4YY

ISBN 978-0-521-18158-7 Paperback American English edition

To my mother Eve, Janet and Christoffer, my rock.

Illustrations by Jose Rubio

Exercises by hypen

Contents

Prologue   An interesting summer   5

Chapter 1   I don't want to go!   6

Chapter 2   Two hundred stores   10

Chapter 3   We wait and we watch   18

Chapter 4   Ms. Averly's cabin   23

Chapter 5   Now or never!   30

Chapter 6   Summer sounds   36

People in the story

Katy: a 13-year-old girl at summer camp[1]
Mom: Katy's mom
Dad: Katy's dad
Ms. Averly: the director of the summer camp
Riley: a 14-year-old boy at summer camp
George: the bus driver at the summer camp

BEFORE YOU READ

● ●

1 Look at the pictures in Chapters 1 and 2. What do you think? Answer the questions.

1 How does Katy feel in Chapter 1?

....

2 What is strange about the campers?

....

An interesting summer

"It's finished," the first person said.

"Good! And then they forget everything?" the second person asked.

"Everything."

"Very good!" the second person said with a smile. "It's going to be an *interesting* summer!"

Chapter 1

I don't want to go!

"I'm not going!" Katy shouted. "I'm not!"

Katy sat at the kitchen table. She was angry. "I'm NOT going to camp!"

"Don't shout at me, Katy." Now Katy's mom was angry, too.

Her dad stopped reading his e-book. "Katy, say you're sorry to your mom," he said.

Katy looked down at her cereal. "I'm sorry, Mom."

Then she looked up at her dad. "Dad, please, try to understand. I'm *13* now. Thirteen-year-old girls don't go to summer camp. They play sports. They play computer games. They go out with their friends. They go shopping. They don't go to camp! Please, Dad, please! I hate camp. It's –"

THUD! Katy's dad put his coffee cup on the table. "Oh, Katy. Stop! We understand – you don't want to go."

"Katy, look at this," her mom said. The camp Web site was on her computer.

"There's a beautiful lake next to the camp. You can go swimming every day. You love swimming."

Katy wasn't interested. "Mom, I can't go swimming. I've got an earache[2]." Katy put her hand on her ear.

"Earache? When did that start?" her mom asked.

"She doesn't have an earache," Katy's dad said. "But she's giving *me* a headache!" He started laughing and Katy's mom smiled.

Katy didn't laugh. "I *have* an earache!" And she put her hand over her ear again.

Katy's mom started reading the Web site. "Three or four times a week, our campers go on visits to interesting places like museums[3] and the zoo. They can also visit some big shopping malls. Campers can –"

"But Mom, I hate . . . what did you say?" Katy *loved* shopping and she was interested now. She stopped talking and looked at the computer.

Katy's mom and dad said nothing. Five minutes later, Katy stood up.

"OK," she said. "When do I leave?"

*   *   *

The bus stopped in front of a big cabin[4] and the campers got off. A woman stood in front of them. She looked important, but she smiled.

"Welcome to Camp Idlewood," the woman said. "My name's Ms. Averly and I'm the camp director. You met George, the driver. And these are some of our helpers." Katy looked at the campers. There was a boy next to her. He had a lollipop in his mouth.

"I knew it. They're all babies at camp," Katy thought.

"And please take them to George. Thank you!" Ms. Averly stopped talking and walked away.

"Take what?" Katy thought. "What did she say?"

"Excuse me," Katy said to the boy with the lollipop. "What did Ms. Averly say? Did you hear?"

"Of course I did," he said. He looked angry.

"Why is he angry with me? I only asked him a question," Katy thought. She looked at the boy. His baseball cap said "Riley."

She tried again. "Sorry, what did Ms. Averly say?"

The boy with the lollipop didn't reply. He didn't look at Katy, and he didn't answer her question.

"Riley?" Katy said again. "Is that your name?"

The boy said nothing.

"Riley Jones," one of the camp helpers shouted. "Riley Jones. Are you here?"

The boy still didn't say anything.

"Hey!" Katy said. And she pulled the boy's arm.

"What? What do you want?" the boy said.

"I think they're calling your name."

"What?" said the boy. "Oh, yeah, I know." He walked over to the helper. They talked for a minute, and the boy looked at Katy.

"Stupid boy and his stupid lollipops," Katy said. "Why did I come here?"

Chapter 2

Two hundred stores

Katy ran to the bus. She was happy. Today there was a visit to a museum and then . . . a mall! She still had an earache, but she didn't want to say anything about it.

She got on the bus. There was only one place to sit. It was next to Riley, the stupid boy with his stupid lollipops.

"Hi," Riley said. "I'm sorry about the other day. I wasn't very nice."

A lollipop was in his hand. "Do you want a lollipop?" he asked.

Katy didn't say anything. She was still a little angry with Riley, but he was very nice today. She took the lollipop and sat down next to him.

They talked and talked. They liked the same books and computer games, music, and movies. After an hour on the bus, they were good friends.

The campers on the bus also talked and laughed. They made a lot of noise.

"Are you OK?" Riley asked. Katy's hand was over her ear.

"It's the noise. Please don't tell anyone, but I've got an earache. I don't want to see the doctor. I want to go to the mall," Katy said.

Riley looked at Katy for a minute. "I need to tell *you* something, too. I can't hear very well. I'm a little deaf[5]."

"What? But you can hear me," Katy said.

"I can also read lips," Riley replied. "And I sometimes put this in my ear. But its not very nice to wear." He had something small in his hand. It was a hearing aid[6].

"Wow!" Katy said. She looked at the camp director. Ms. Averly was at the front of the bus next to George. "What's Ms. Averly saying now?"

"She's telling George about the mall. She's saying that there are 200 stores."

"Wow!" Katy said again.

The bus stopped. They were at the museum. George and Ms. Averly gave everyone an MP3 player.

Katy looked at Riley. "MP3 players? Are we going to listen to music?"

"We're going to use these MP3 players on our visits," Ms. Averly said. "They have lots of information[7] about the things in the museums and malls. Please try them now."

Katy and Riley tried their MP3 players.

"This isn't good for my earache," Katy said to Riley. "I can't use it, and I can't say why not!"

Riley took Katy's MP3 player and pushed some buttons on it.

"Try it now," he said.

"Hey. There's no sound. I can't hear anything on it now. What did you do?" Katy said.

Riley smiled. "Maybe I'm not a stupid boy with stupid lollipops," he said.

Katy looked at Riley and laughed. "You read my lips!" she said. "On the first day!"

"Of course," Riley said, and he smiled.

"Are your MP3 players working?" Ms. Averly asked everyone.

"Yes!" everyone on the bus replied. Katy and Riley shouted "Yes!" too.

"OK. Let's go!" Ms. Averly got off the bus and walked into the museum.

The visit was short. After half an hour, they were on the bus again. Fifteen minutes later, they stopped at a very big mall.

Ms. Averly spoke. "Campers, there are 200 stores here. Please meet at the bus in two hours."

Katy wanted to run into the mall, but the other campers were very slow.

For over an hour, Katy and Riley went to lots of stores. They looked at DVDs, books, computer games . . . everything!

In a sports store, Riley turned to Katy. "Why aren't you buying anything?" he asked. "You love shopping."

"Yes, but first I look in *all* the stores."

"Me, too! We're going to be very good friends!" Riley laughed.

Later, they went into a music store.

"Hey, look," Riley said. "They're from our camp."
Riley and Katy watched the campers.

"That's strange[8]," Riley said.

"What?" Katy asked. "They aren't doing anything."

"Yes. That's it! They aren't doing *anything*," he said again. "They're just standing there and listening to their MP3 players."

"Look! There's George. He's watching the campers, too," Katy said.

"Hmm . . . strange campers and a strange bus driver. Very interesting," Riley said.

"You watch too much TV!" Katy laughed. "Come on. We need to go back now."

"Leave your bags and backpacks here in front of the bus, please," Ms. Averly said to the campers. "George can put them on the bus. At camp, go to dinner. George is going to take your bags to your cabins."

On the bus, Katy looked out the window. "George is doing something with my backpack."

"He's just putting it on the bus," Riley said.

"Maybe you're right," Katy said.

She turned to the girl behind her.

"Hello," she said. "What did you buy?"

"I don't know," the girl replied.

"I don't understand," Katy said. "What did you get at the mall?"

"I don't know," the girl said again.

Katy looked at Riley. "Now that *is* strange!" Katy stopped speaking. There wasn't a sound on the bus. She looked at the boys and girls. They were all quiet.

"And why is it quiet now? What's wrong with everyone?"

LOOKING BACK

● ●

1 Check your answers to *Before you read* on page 4.

ACTIVITIES

● ●

2 Complete the sentences with the names in the box.

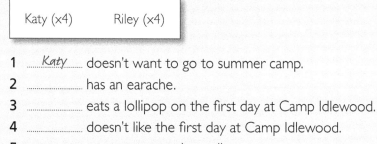

Katy (x4)   Riley (x4)

1 ......*Katy*....... doesn't want to go to summer camp.

2 .... has an earache.

3 .... eats a lollipop on the first day at Camp Idlewood.

4 .... doesn't like the first day at Camp Idlewood.

5 .... wants to go to the mall.

6 .... can't hear very well.

7 .... has a hearing aid.

8 .... can read people's lips.

3 <u>Underline</u> the correct words in each sentence.

1 Katy thinks that 13-year-old girls *go* / <u>*don't go*</u>
   to summer camp.

2 Katy's mom tells her to look at a Web site about a
   summer camp / *shopping mall*.

3 Katy's dad *thinks* / *doesn't think* she has an earache.

4 *George* / *Ms. Averly* is the director of Camp Idlewood.

5 Katy tells *nobody* / *Riley* about her earache.

6 Katy and Riley *think* / *don't think* that George and some of
   the campers are strange.

4 Who or what do the <u>underlined</u> words refer to in these lines from the text?

MP3 players	Camp Idlewood	the campers
Ms. Averly	Katy and Riley	K̶a̶t̶y̶'̶s̶ ̶m̶o̶m̶ ̶a̶n̶d̶ ̶d̶a̶d̶

1 "Oh, Katy. Stop! <u>We</u> understand –" (page 7)

Katy's mom and dad

2 "What did <u>she</u> say?" (page 8) ....

3 "Why did I come <u>here</u>?" (page 9) ....

4 Please try <u>them</u> now. (page 12) ....

5 Later <u>they</u> went into a music store. (page 13)

....

6 "<u>They</u>'re from our camp." (page 14) ....

5 Answer the questions.

1 Why is Katy's mom angry?

....

2 Why doesn't Riley answer the camp helpers?

....

3 Why are Katy and Riley going to be good friends?

....

LOOKING FORWARD

• •

6 Check (✓) the things you think are true in Chapters 3 and 4.

1 Katy leaves Camp Idlewood. ☐

2 Katy and Riley see the campers taking things. ☐

Chapter 3

We wait and we watch

After dinner, Riley and Katy walked down to the lake.

"OK," Riley said. "There are some strange things at this camp – the campers in the mall, George, the girl on the bus. And why was everyone quiet? I think that –"

"Shh! I can hear someone," Katy said.

The two friends saw a person near the boathouse, next to the lake.

"It's George!" Katy said. "He's talking to someone on the phone."

They watched from behind a tree.

"Riley, can you read George's lips?" Katy asked.

"I can try," Riley answered.

They stopped talking. After two or three minutes, George walked away.

"What did he say?" asked Katy.

"I don't know. I didn't understand everything – only 'backpacks . . . Ms. Averly doesn't know . . . summer sounds . . . tomorrow'. "

Katy didn't say anything.

"We're going to the Science Center tomorrow. I think we can only wait and watch," Riley said.

Katy smiled. "OK, we wait . . . and we watch."

*   *   *

The next day, the campers went to the Science Center. They all got MP3 players again. Riley took Katy's MP3 player.

"Katy, look. Push these buttons and you don't hear anything," Riley said.

Twenty minutes later, they sat down. "Well, I don't see anything strange," Riley said. "But I love the Science Center!"

"Me, too!" Katy said. "Everyone is quiet, but that's all. We can watch them again at the mall."

Then Riley saw George behind them.

"Shh, don't talk," he said to Katy. "George is watching us. Take a lollipop, get up, and go."

Katy got up, took a lollipop, and walked over to a group of campers.

The visit to the Science Center finished, and the bus took them to a new mall.

"You have two hours!" Ms. Averly said.

Katy and Riley walked behind the other campers. Three boys went into a camera store. One camper talked to the salesperson. Two looked around the store. Katy didn't see anything strange.

"They're just looking in stores," she told Riley.

She wanted to leave, but Riley wanted to wait a little.

"Look again, Katy," Riley said.

One camper was still with the salesperson. Two campers were near some cameras. They took two cameras and then put only *one* camera back.

"Did you see that?" Riley asked Katy. "They took two cameras, but –"

"They only put *one* back!" Katy finished.

"They're taking cameras, Katy."

"They're *stealing*[9] cameras," Katy said.

"Come on," Riley said. "We need to find some other campers."

Katy and Riley left the camera store and looked around the mall. They found three campers in an expensive sunglasses store and some more in a computer games store. In both stores, they saw the same thing.

"They're all stealing!" Riley said.

"This is very bad, Riley!" Katy said. "One camper talks to the salesperson, and two other campers steal something. And they're good at it!"

"I don't understand," Riley said. "Why is everyone stealing?"

"I don't know," Katy replied. "But those campers are coming over here. And they aren't happy!"

"Of course they aren't happy. We saw them!" Riley said. "And they know it."

"What are we going to do?" Katy asked.

"I don't know," Riley said. "And what are *they* going to do to *us*?"

Chapter 4

Ms. Averly's cabin

Katy and Riley waited for one of the campers to say something, but they didn't stop. They just walked out of the store. Katy and Riley watched them.

"Phew! They didn't do anything." Riley looked at Katy. "What's it all about?"

"I don't know, Riley," Katy said. "But we can talk about it on the bus."

She looked at her watch. "It's time to go," she said.

"Wait," Riley said, and he took two computer games.

"Buy a game," he said. "All the campers have things in their backpacks. George needs to see something in our backpacks, too."

They bought the computer games and walked quickly to the bus. George took their backpacks, and they got on the bus. The bus was very quiet again driving back to camp. Katy and Riley were quiet, too. They needed to think. They had lots of questions.

"We need to tell Ms. Averly," Katy said after a long time. "We have to tell her everything – everything we saw yesterday and today."

"Maybe you're right. She's the camp director," Riley said. "We can go see her after dinner."

The two friends had dinner and went to Ms. Averly's cabin. They pushed the door and it opened.

"She has to be here," Riley said.

"Ms. Averly?" Katy called. "Are you here?" There was no answer. Katy turned to leave, but Riley stopped her.

"Come on," he said and walked into the cabin. "Maybe she can't hear us." Katy wasn't very happy, but she walked in, too.

"Wow!" he said. "Look at that computer!"

There was a computer on Ms. Averly's desk. It looked very expensive. Riley walked across the room and walked into the desk.

"Ouch!" he said.

The three computer screens turned on[10].

"Riley! What are you doing?" Katy said. She was still by the door. She didn't want to be in the cabin. "Ms. Averly isn't going to like this."

"I just want to look at her computer. It must be very expensive," Riley said. "It's a . . ."

Riley stopped talking. "Hey, what's this?" he asked. "Katy, close the door and come here. You need to see this."

"What, Riley? What is it?" Katy asked. She closed the door and walked over to the computer. On the screen, there was a Web site.

"I don't know. What do *you* think it is?" Riley asked. He put a lollipop in his mouth.

Katy looked at the Web site.

"Wait a minute. There's a video," Riley put his lollipop on the desk. He clicked the play button on the video.

Katy and Riley watched the video. It was about a scientist.

"I can't hear everything," Riley said. "What's he saying?"

"The man with the black glasses is a scientist," Katy replied. "He plays strange sounds to animals. The animals learn things from the sounds."

She stopped the video. "Why did Ms. Averly watch this?"

"I don't know," Riley said. He clicked the button again and the video started.

They watched for a minute, and then Katy spoke.

"It says Mr. Black Glasses has one problem. The animals forget everything after a short time. He's working on this problem now. One day, Mr. Black Glasses wants to use these sounds on people. He thinks people can learn new things by listening to them." The video stopped.

"But I still don't understand. Why does Ms. Averly like this video?"

"Maybe she's got a dog," Riley said. "I don't know."

But then he started to smile. "Wait! I think I know. She's trying to –"

Katy stopped him. "Wait. You can tell me later. We need to leave. Ms. Averly isn't going to be happy."

"You're right," Riley said.

They walked to the door and opened it.

"Aah!" they shouted.

"What are you doing in here?" a woman said.

It was Ms. Averly!

LOOKING BACK

●●

1 Check your answers to *Looking forward* on page 17.

ACTIVITIES

●●●

2 Put the sentences in order.
1 Katy and Riley meet Ms. Averly in her cabin. ☐
2 Katy wants to tell Ms. Averly about the strange things at Camp Idlewood. ☐
3 Katy and Riley watch a video about a scientist. ☐
4 Katy and Riley see somebody near the boathouse. 1
5 Katy and Riley don't see anything strange at the Science Center. ☐
6 Ms. Averly's computer screen turns on. ☐
7 Riley tries to read George's lips at the lake. ☐

3 Are the sentences true (*T*) or false (*F*)?
1 Katy and Riley see Ms. Averly near the lake. F
2 Riley understands everything George says on the phone. ☐
3 George watches Katy and Riley at the Science Center. ☐
4 One camper talks to the salesperson, and two other campers steal something. ☐
5 All the campers are quiet on the bus. ☐
6 Riley didn't want to turn on Ms. Averly's computer. ☐
7 Mr. Black Glasses thinks people can learn new things from some sounds. ☐

4 Match the questions with the answers.

1 What do the campers get at the Science Center? $\boxed{b}$
2 Who do Katy and Riley watch? ☐
3 What do Katy and Riley give George? ☐
4 What's on Ms. Averly's computer screens? ☐

a Backpacks.
~~b~~ MP3 players.
c A video about a scientist.
d The campers.

5 <u>Underline</u> the correct words in each sentence.

1 At the lake, <u>*Riley*</u> / *Katy* talks about the strange things at Camp Idlewood.
2 Some campers steal *a camera* / *two cameras*.
3 Katy and Riley know that *all the* / *some* campers are stealing at the mall.
4 The campers *say something* / *don't say anything* to Katy and Riley.
5 Katy and Riley *buy* / *steal* computer games and put them in their backpacks.
6 Mr. Black Glasses plays strange sounds to *animals* / *people*.

LOOKING FORWARD

6 Check (✓) the things you think are true in the final two chapters.

1 Katy and Riley call the police and tell them about the stealing. ☐
2 George helps Mr. Black Glasses do bad things. ☐

Chapter 5

Now or never!

"What are you doing in my cabin?" the camp director asked again.

Katy spoke first. "Oh! Ms. Averly! We wanted to tell you about some strange –"

Riley stopped her. "It was me, Ms. Averly! I'm very sorry. It was a game. We were only here for a minute."

Ms. Averly was very angry. She looked in the cabin.

"You can't come in here," she shouted. "Do I need to call your parents?"

"Oh, no, please don't call them. We're very sorry," Riley answered.

Ms. Averly looked at Katy. "Katy? Did you want to say something?"

Katy looked at her feet. "I, um, no, but I'm sorry, too."

Ms. Averly waited and thought. Then she spoke. "Come with me, you two."

The two friends walked with Ms. Averly across the camp and to the kitchen.

"These two campers are going to help you tonight," Ms. Averly said to the kitchen workers.

She turned to Katy and Riley. "Go back to your cabins after you finish here. Do you understand? *Your* cabins!"

"Yes, Ms. Averly," they answered.

Katy and Riley started cleaning the kitchen. They didn't talk.

An hour later, they walked back to their cabins.

"They're using the MP3 players," Riley said, putting a lollipop in his mouth.

"Oh, Riley, I'm too tired to talk. I just want to go to bed," Katy said.

"But listen, Katy," Riley said. "This is important. George and Ms. Averly are using the MP3 players on all of us!"

"What? How do you know?"

"Think about the video, Katy. Ms. Averly and Mr. Black Glasses are doing the same thing," Riley said.

"I didn't see any MP3 players in the video. It was about strange sounds and animals."

"The strange sounds are *on* the MP3 players, Katy!" Riley said. "The campers listen to the sounds, steal things, and then forget everything! Didn't you see? In the stores, all the campers had MP3 players."

Riley waited, but Katy didn't say anything.

"Shh! Someone's coming," Katy said. "I can hear them. Can you see anyone?" she asked.

"There!" Riley said. "It's Ms. Averly and George. Can you hear them? I can't read their lips – it's too dark."

"Yes, I can." The night was quiet and Katy heard everything.

After a minute she turned and said, "It *is* Ms. Averly and George! And they *are* using the MP3 players! I heard them."

"What did they say?" Riley asked.

"They're going to watch us tomorrow. Ms. Averly knows we aren't stealing, and she doesn't understand the problem," Katy said. "George thinks our MP3 players don't work. He says that she has to call her 'friend.' "

She looked at Riley. "We need to go to the police."

"What can we say?" Riley asked. "The police aren't going to listen to two teenagers with a stupid story about strange sounds and MP3 players."

"You're right. We need to find something," Katy said. "Then we go to the police, OK?"

* * *

The next morning, Katy and Riley walked to the bus. Today's visit was to the city zoo. Ms. Averly was in front of the bus.

"Good morning, Ms. Averly," Katy said.

"Hello, you two," Ms. Averly replied. She smiled at them.

"We're very sorry about yesterday, um, in your cabin," Katy said.

"That's OK," she smiled. "Enjoy your day today."

At the zoo, Katy and Riley didn't talk. Ms. Averly or George was near them all the time.

Later, in the mall, it was the same – Ms. Averly or George was always behind them.

"Watch the campers and copy them," Katy told Riley.

"What?" Riley said. "Katy, they're stealing! Are we going to steal, too?"

Katy didn't answer.

They went into a watch store. Ms. Averly watched them. Katy looked at the watches. George came and spoke to Ms. Averly, and she left. Katy and Riley waited. They were very afraid.

Riley had an expensive watch in his hand. "We can't wait, Katy. Open your backpack. It's now or never."

"I think never," said a man behind them.

Chapter 6

Summer sounds

Katy and Riley turned round. It was George!

"Quick!" he said. "Take these."

George had two shopping bags. They had lots of things in them. Katy and Riley didn't do anything.

"I'm trying to help you!" George said.

Katy looked into his eyes. She put one of the shopping bags in her backpack.

Riley looked at her. "What are you doing?"

"Take it, Riley. I think it's OK."

"Quick! We can talk later!" George said and gave Riley the second bag.

"Now go to the bus. Wait for me in your cabins after dinner. I *am* helping you!" George said, and he walked away.

At the bus, George didn't speak to them. He took their backpacks and the friends got on.

Riley watched from the window. "Look! Ms. Averly's talking to George," he said.

Katy was too afraid to look.

"She's looking in our backpacks," Riley said. "And she's smiling! We did it!"

"No, Riley. *George* did it," Katy said. "He helped us."

The bus got to camp, and Riley asked, "What now?"

"We have dinner, go to our cabins, and then wait for George. That's all we can do," Katy replied.

They went to their cabins after dinner. Katy opened her door. It was very dark. She heard a sound.

"Hello?" she said slowly.

Someone put a hand over Katy's mouth.

Ten minutes later, Katy opened her eyes. She was in the boathouse, near the lake. Riley was next to her. He looked afraid. The boathouse door opened. Ms. Averly and George walked in.

"I didn't see anything strange at the mall today. Their backpacks had lots of things in them," George said.

"But I found this next to my computer." Ms. Averly had a lollipop in her hand.

Katy looked at Riley. "He left a lollipop on the desk!" she thought.

"They looked at my computer. They must know everything!" Ms. Averly said.

Her phone rang. She answered it, "We're in the boathouse. Where are you? . . . OK. See you in a minute. Bye."

"Was that your friend?" George asked.

Ms. Averly walked over to Katy and Riley. "Yes, he's coming now. Tomorrow is going to be a sad day."

"A sad day?" George asked.

"Yes. Teenagers can sometimes be very stupid. They go swimming late at night in the lake and . . . we never see them again," Ms. Averly finished.

"I understand," George said.

"Yes. They know too much," a man said from the door of the boathouse.

Ms. Averly and George turned around. Katy looked at Riley. It was Mr. Black Glasses! The man in the video.

"The sounds on the MP3 players are yours? You made them?" George asked the scientist.

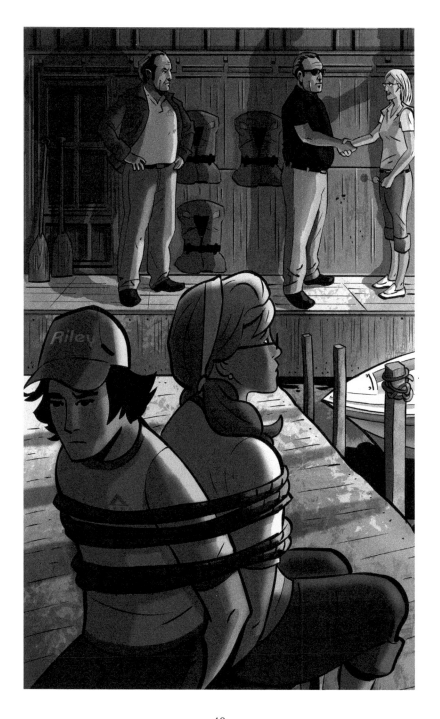

"Yes. And this summer is just the start. Think of the things we can do with my sounds!" Mr. Black Glasses replied.

"Summer sounds," George said. "*Summer sounds!*"

"Why did he say that?" thought Katy.

George was close to the teenagers now.

A second later, there was a loud[11] noise, and the door of the boathouse opened. Ms. Averly and Mr. Black Glasses turned around.

"Police! Hands up!" someone shouted.

Ms. Averly and Mr. Black Glasses put their hands up slowly. George started to help Katy and Riley. "My name's George Cooper. I'm a police officer," he said. "You're OK now."

*   *   *

Katy and Riley sat on a police car with George next to them. Two police officers left with Ms. Averly and Mr. Black Glasses in another car.

"But I don't understand," Riley said. "You knew about Ms. Averly. Why didn't you stop her?"

"Ms. Averly wasn't important," George replied. "She was only the scientist's helper. We needed to stop *him*. He never visited the camp. But tonight he needed to come. Thanks to you, he's never going to use his sounds again."

"How did the other police officers know that Mr. Black Glasses, um, the scientist, was here?" Katy asked.

"I had a microphone in my jacket. I said 'summer sounds' and the police came in," George answered with a smile.

Riley looked at George. "Summer sounds! You said that at the lake!

"Did you hear me by the lake?" George asked. "But there wasn't anyone there!"

"I'm a little deaf," Riley smiled. "I read your lips."

There was the noise of a car, and Katy turned around. "My parents!" she said.

Katy's mom and dad ran to their daughter.

"Katy! Are you OK?" her mom asked.

"I'm all right, Mom."

"We're very sorry, Katy. You didn't want to come to this camp. We can go home tonight," Katy's mom said.

"But I can't go home now, Mom," Katy said.

"Why? Do the police need you?" Katy's dad looked at George.

"No, we don't need –" George started.

"I don't *want* to go home now," said Katy. "Riley and I saw lots of things in the stores. But we didn't buy anything nice! We want to go shopping!"

LOOKING BACK

• •

1 Check your answers to *Looking forward* on page 29.

ACTIVITIES

• •

2 Complete the sentences with the names in the box.

> George (x2)   Ms. Averly and George
>
> Mr. Black Glasses   Ms. Averly

1 Katy doesn't tell *Ms. Averly* about the strange things at Camp Idlewood.

2 Riley thinks .... use the MP3 players on all the campers.

3 .... helps Katy and Riley at the mall.

4 .... tells Ms. Averly that he's coming to the boathouse.

5 .... is a police officer.

3 Match the questions with the answers.

1 How does Ms. Averly feel about Katy and Riley in her cabin? [c]

2 Why don't Katy and Riley go to the police? [ ]

3 Why do Katy and Riley see Ms. Averly smile near the bus? [ ]

4 Why is George interested in Mr. Black Glasses? [ ]

5 How do the police know Mr. Black Glasses is at the boathouse? [ ]

a They won't listen to the story.

b He can do many bad things with his sounds.

c She gets very angry.

d He has a microphone in his jacket.

e They have many things in their backpacks.

44

4 Are the sentences true (*T*) or false (*F*)?

1 Riley thinks that the MP3 players play strange sounds. ☐T☐

2 The campers hear strange sounds in the bus. ☐

3 The campers steal things and then forget. ☐

4 Ms. Averly or George watches Katy and Riley at the city zoo and the mall. ☐

5 Katy and Riley almost steal an expensive watch. ☐

6 Mr. Black Glasses is going to use the animal sounds again. ☐

7 Ms. Averly makes the strange sounds on the MP3 players. ☐

5 <u>Underline</u> the correct words in each sentence.

1 Katy and Riley *tell* / <u>*don't tell*</u> Ms. Averly what they are doing in her cabin.

2 Ms. Averly *calls* / *doesn't call* Katy's and Riley's parents.

3 *Ms. Averly* / *George* doesn't know why Katy and Riley aren't stealing.

4 George gives Katy and Riley *two bags* / *an expensive watch*.

5 Ms. Averly takes Katy and Riley to *the boathouse* / *her cabin*.

6 Katy wants to *leave Camp Idlewood* / *go shopping*.

6 Answer the questions.

1 Who hears Ms. Averly and George talking about the MP3 players?

....

2 Why don't Katy and Riley steal at the end of Chapter 5?

....

3 What does Riley leave in Ms. Averly's cabin?

....

4 Who is Ms. Averly's "friend"?

....

Glossary

[1]**summer camp** (page 4) *noun*   somewhere children and teenagers can stay in the summer and play sports, games, etc.

[2]**earache** (page 7) *noun*   a pain or bad feeling in your ear

[3]**museum** (page 7) *noun*   somewhere you go to look at important things about art, history, science, etc.

[4]**cabin** (page 8) *noun*   a small house

[5]**deaf** (page 10) *adjective*   a deaf person cannot hear

[6]**hearing aid** (page 11) *noun*   something that helps **deaf** people hear

[7]**information** (page 12) *noun*   things that you read, hear, etc. about something or someone

[8]**strange** (page 14) *adjective*   something that is not usual

[9]**to steal** (page 21) *verb*   to take and keep something that is not yours

[10]**to turn on** *(page 24) phrasal verb*   make a computer, light, etc. start working

[11]**loud** (page 41) *adjective*   If something or somebody is loud, they make a lot of noise.